Mark McGwire

by Phelan Powell

Reading Consultant:
Dr. Robert Miller
Professor of Special Education
Minnesota State University

CAPSTONE BOOKS

an imprint of Capstone Press
Mankato, Minnesota

Capstone Books are published by Capstone Press
151 Good Counsel Drive, P.O. Box 669, Mankato, Minnesota 56002
http://www.capstone-press.com

Library of Congress Cataloging-in-Publication Data
Powell, Phelan.
    Mark McGwire/by Phelan Powell.
    p. cm.—(Sports heroes)
    Includes bibliographical references (p. 43) and index.
    Summary: Presents a biography of the St. Louis Cardinal power hitter who broke Roger Maris's single-season home run record in 1998.
    ISBN 0-7368-0578-8
    1. McGwire, Mark, 1963—Juvenile literature. 2. Baseball players—United States—Biography—Juvenile literature. [1. McGwire, Mark, 1963– 2. Baseball players.] I. Title. II. Sports heroes (Mankato, Minn.)
    GV865.M3123 P69 2001
    796.357'092—dc21
[B]   00-023628

Editorial Credits
Chuck Miller and Matt Doeden, editors; Timothy Halldin, cover designer and illustrator;
    Heidi Schoof and Kimberly Danger, photo researchers

Photo Credits
Active Images, Inc./Mitchell B. Reibel, 22
Allsport USA/Jed Jacobsohn, 4, 7; Otto Greul, 26
Reuters/Sue Ogrocki/Archive Photos, 35
SportsChrome-USA, 25; SportsChrome-USA/Rob Tringali Jr., cover, 12, 14, 29,
    36, 44; Scott Cunningham, 9, 40; Jeff Carlick, 10, 20, 38; Louis Raynor, 31,
    32; Steve Woltman, 47
USC Athletics, 16, 19

1 2 3 4 5 6 06 05 04 03 02 01

Table of Contents

CHAPTER 1

Breaking the Record

On September 8, 1998, Major League Baseball fans filled every seat at Busch Stadium in St. Louis. There, the St. Louis Cardinals were playing the Chicago Cubs. Millions more fans watched the game on their TV sets. Most of the fans were watching St. Louis Cardinals' first baseman Mark McGwire. Mark had already hit 61 home runs during the season. He needed one more home run to break the record set by Roger Maris in 1961.

Mark had been under pressure for the whole season. He had hit 57 home runs in 1997. Fans

Mark hugged his son, Matthew, after he broke the home-run record.

> My heart was beating a thousand miles a minute, and I was just telling myself to get a good pitch to hit.
> —Mark McGwire, *The New York Times*, 9/8/98

and members of the media had known all season that Mark could break the record. He had faced excited reporters and fans throughout the 1998 season. He also was under pressure from Cubs' outfielder Sammy Sosa. Sosa also was chasing the home-run record. He had hit 58 home runs so far that year. Fans and members of the media tried to guess all season which player would break the record.

In the fourth inning, Mark stepped to home plate to face Cubs' pitcher Steve Trachsel. Mark took a few practice swings and got into his batting stance. Moments later, Mark hit Trachsel's pitch over the left field wall. It was home run number 62. Mark had broken the record.

The fans stood and cheered. Mark was so excited that he almost forgot to touch first base as he rounded the bases. Cubs' players even shook Mark's hand as he passed them.

Mark's 10-year-old son, Matthew, was waiting to hug him when he reached home plate. Matthew was wearing a Cardinals

Millions of fans around the world watched as Mark hit his 62nd home run.

uniform. He was one of the team's bat boys. Sosa also came in from the outfield to congratulate Mark. Both players were relieved that one of them had finally broken the record. The next day, newspapers throughout North America had photos of Mark on their front pages.

About Mark McGwire

Mark has been a baseball player most of his life. He began playing in grade school and has been a major league player since 1986. He has always been known as a great home-run hitter. Mark also has been recognized as a very good defensive player.

Mark also tries to make a difference off the field. He works with a variety of children's charities. He makes public appearances and gives money to help sick children. He uses his popularity to give attention to various children's causes.

CAREER STATISTICS

Mark McGwire

Major League Batting Statistics

Year	Team	Games	Avg	HR	RBI
1986	OAK	18	.189	3	9
1987	OAK	151	.289	49	118
1988	OAK	155	.260	32	99
1989	OAK	143	.231	33	95
1990	OAK	156	.235	39	108
1991	OAK	154	.201	22	75
1992	OAK	139	.268	42	104
1993	OAK	27	.333	9	24
1994	OAK	47	.252	9	25
1995	OAK	104	.274	39	90
1996	OAK	130	.312	52	113
1997	OAK/STL	156	.274	58	123
1998	STL	155	.299	70	147
1999	STL	153	.278	65	147
Career		1,688	.265	522	1,277

CHAPTER 2

The Early Years

Mark was born October 1, 1963, in Pomona, California. His parents are John and Ginger McGwire. John was a dentist. Ginger had once worked as a nurse. Mark is the second of John and Ginger's five sons.

An Athletic Family

All of Mark's brothers were good athletes growing up. Mike is the oldest brother. He played golf and soccer during high school. Bobby is the middle brother. He also played golf and soccer during high school. Dan is the fourth brother. He was a football star in high

Mark grew up in California.

Mark knew at an early age that he wanted to be a baseball player.

school and college. Dan even played backup quarterback in the National Football League. He played for the Seattle Seahawks and the Miami Dolphins. Jay is the youngest brother. Jay was a defensive tackle on his high school's football team. But Jay suffered an eye injury during high school. The injury ended his football career. Jay became a weight lifter and a bodybuilding expert instead.

Mark began playing football in grade school. But he soon decided that he did not like football. He did not like practicing all week for only one game.

Mark decided to play baseball instead. He began as a pitcher. But Mark's Little League coaches saw that he had great power. They wanted Mark to practice his hitting. Mark decided to do both.

High School

Mark played baseball for Damien High School. But he sometimes had trouble seeing the ball. He had worn glasses almost all of his life. In high school, Mark got contact lenses. This corrected his vision. His baseball skills improved with his corrected vision.

Mark watched baseball when he was not playing. He and his friends were fans of the California Angels. The Angels played their home games in Anaheim. Mark did not have a favorite player like many of his friends did.

Instead, Mark watched all the players. He tried to watch what each player did well.

Mark's father noticed Mark's skills and attention to baseball. He thought that Mark had a natural understanding of the game. He believed Mark might someday be able to play in the major leagues. John sent Mark to a baseball clinic when Mark was 14. The clinic was called Cal Poly Pomona. There, Mark learned how to improve his baseball skills. Many of the coaches at the clinic noticed his talent. They also saw how hard he worked to get better.

Mark continued to be a star for Damien High School. He had a career batting average of .359. Mark also pitched for the team. His ERA was 1.90. Mark earned a second-team All-California Interscholastic Federation Award in his senior year. Damien's baseball team also went to the state tournament. Mark had a .415 batting average, 53 Runs Batted In (RBIs), and 14 home runs that season.

Mark always had a powerful swing.

CHAPTER 3

Growing Skills

Mark impressed people with his senior season on Damien's baseball team. Many colleges and universities offered Mark scholarships to play for their baseball teams. The University of Southern California (USC) was one of them. USC had a great baseball history. The university had won more national championships in baseball than any other college team. Major league players such as Tom Seaver, Dave Kingman, and Steve Kemp had played for USC. USC also was close to Mark's home.

Mark earned a scholarship to play for the University of Southern California.

Mark wanted to go to USC. But his decision was not easy. The Montreal Expos selected Mark in the eighth round of the 1981 Major League Baseball draft. Mark had to decide between college and professional baseball.

The Expos offered Mark $8,500 to join their organization. But Mark would have to start in the minor leagues. He knew it might take years to reach the majors. There was even a chance that he would never reach them. Mark figured that the scholarship to USC was worth about $50,000. He decided that he wanted to attend college. He hoped to play in the major leagues after he finished college.

College Ball

Mark's first season at USC was difficult. His batting average was .200. He hit only three home runs with 11 RBIs. A USC coach named Ron Vaughn decided to help Mark improve his skills. Vaughn took Mark to play in the Alaskan Summer League in Anchorage, Alaska. Vaughn asked Mark to play first base

Mark became one of the best hitters on the USC team during his second year.

Mark was drafted by the Oakland A's in 1984.

for the Glacier Pilots in Anchorage. Vaughn believed Mark's future was as a power hitter. Vaughn wanted Mark to get as many at-bats as he could.

Mark missed his family and friends while he was in Alaska. But he knew that the experience would make him a better player. Mark practiced and played hard that summer. He became more comfortable at the plate.

Mark's improvement showed quickly. He became one of the best hitters for USC. In 1983, Mark hit 32 home runs. No player in the PAC-10 conference had ever hit that many. In 1984, *The Sporting News* named Mark the College Player of the Year.

The Olympics

In 1983, the U.S. Baseball Federation selected Mark to play on its pre-Olympic team. This team played baseball games leading up to the 1984 Olympics in Los Angeles, California.

Mark and his teammates toured the United States. They also played in countries such as China and Japan. Mark helped the team to a second-place finish in the International Cup Games in Belgium. Mark also was an important player in the Pan-American Games in Venezuela. Mark had a .454 batting average there. He also hit six home runs.

The U.S. baseball team next played at the 1984 Summer Olympics. The U.S. team played well and advanced to the gold-medal

game. But the team lost to Japan's team. Mark and his teammates received silver medals.

Major League Dreams

Mark's play in the Olympics gained him more than a silver medal. Major league scouts noticed Mark's skills during the Olympics. The Oakland A's and the New York Mets were among the teams who wanted Mark. The A's used the 10th pick in the 1984 draft to select Mark. The A's paid Mark a $125,000 bonus to sign a contract with their organization.

Mark began his professional baseball career in the minor leagues. He started on the A's Class A minor league team in Modesto, California. But Mark did not succeed at first. He was not hitting with as much power as his coaches had expected. Some people believed Mark was not as good a hitter with wooden bats. Mark had used metal bats in college and in the Olympics. Players can swing metal bats with great speed because they are lighter than wooden bats. Mark was having trouble

Mark earned a chance to play for the A's after spending more than a year in the minor leagues.

adjusting to the heavier bats. His batting average was only .200 after his first 16 games.

Mark's coaches sent him down to the A's Instructional League team. There, Mark worked with the team's coaches to adjust. Mark worked hard to improve. He arrived for practice early and stayed until it was too dark to see the ball. Mark's coaches also taught him to play third base. They believed that he could be a successful third baseman in the majors.

Mark's hard work paid off. His coaches sent him back to Modesto. He played well there. In 1986, Mark's coaches moved him up to their Class AA team in Huntsville, Alabama. He batted .303 with 10 home runs in 55 games. In June, Mark began playing for the A's Class AAA team in Tacoma, Washington. In 78 games, he batted .313 and hit 13 home runs. In August, the A's called Mark up to play on their major league team.

Mark began his major league career in 1986.

CHAPTER 4

Big-League Star

Mark played in only 18 major league games in 1986. He played third base. He did not do well. He batted just .189 and hit 3 home runs. It was not the way Mark wanted to begin his major league career.

Rookie of the Year

The A's coaches had confidence in Mark. They knew he was a good hitter and a hard worker. Mark's first full season in the majors was in 1987. His coaches moved him to first base.

Mark started the season strongly. He hit 15 home runs in the month of May. Many people thought he was baseball's most exciting rookie

Mark's coaches moved him to first base in 1987.

player. Sports reporters began asking him for interviews. Fans wanted his autograph.

Mark continued to play well in 1987. He batted .289 and hit a league-leading 49 home runs. No other rookie had ever hit that many. Mark also finished second in the league in RBIs with 118. After the season, he was named American League Rookie of the Year.

Team Success

Mark enjoyed his success in 1987. But the A's were not successful as a team. They did not make the playoffs. Mark helped the team change that in 1988. He batted .260 with 32 home runs. The A's made the playoffs and advanced to the World Series.

Oakland faced the Los Angeles Dodgers in the World Series. Mark helped the A's win game 3 with a ninth-inning home run over the left field fence. But the A's eventually lost the World Series to the Dodgers.

Mark's popularity grew during the 1987 season.

Back problems slowed Mark down early in the 1989 season. His batting average dipped to .231 that year. But he still hit 33 home runs. The A's again made the playoffs and advanced to the World Series. Mark recorded a .343 batting average in the playoffs and the World Series. The A's beat the San Francisco Giants to become the World Series champions.

Ups and Downs

Mark won the Gold Glove award in 1990 for his fielding accomplishments. He hit 39 home runs that year. But he batted only .235.

Mark's batting average dropped to .201 in 1991. Mark thought he might be getting lazy. He decided to start taking better care of his body. Mark's brother Jay designed a training and nutrition program for him. Mark started working out six days a week during the off-season. During the season, he only worked out four days a week. Mark began stretching before and after every game. He also began

Mark won the Gold Glove award in 1990 for his fielding accomplishments.

Only four major league players have hit 200 career home runs in fewer at-bats than Mark.

lifting weights after every game to build up the muscles in his arms and back.

In June 1992, Mark hit his 200th career home run. He hit it in 2,852 at-bats. Only four players in baseball history had hit that many home runs in fewer at-bats. These players were Babe Ruth, Ralph Kiner, Harmon Killebrew, and Eddie Mathews. All of these players had been inducted into Major League Baseball's Hall of Fame.

Mark spent most of 1993 with his left foot in a cast after tearing a tendon during a game. The A's lost 94 games that season. They finished in last place in their division.

Mark suffered from back problems during the first half of 1994. Later that season, he injured his left foot again. The 1994 season ended early. On August 11, all of the major league players went on strike. The players did not think the team owners were treating them fairly.

In 1995, Mark started hitting the ball well again. He hit 39 home runs that season. In 1996, Mark hit 52 home runs. Baseball fans became interested in Mark again. They wondered if he could break Roger Maris's record of 61 home runs in a season.

Changing Teams

In 1997, Mark's contract with the Oakland A's was near its end. He would be a free agent

Wouldn't it be great if we just ended up tied?
I think it would be beautiful.
—Mark McGwire, *The New York Times*, 9-8-98

after the season. He then could play for any team he wanted. The A's knew that they could not afford to sign Mark to another contract. They traded him to the St. Louis Cardinals in the middle of the 1997 season.

Mark was happy about the trade. He felt the Cardinals could be a good team. The Cardinals' fans were happy to have Mark. They cheered loudly whenever he came to bat. Mark ended the 1997 season with 58 home runs.

Baseball fans around the world wondered if Mark would break the home-run record in 1998. He started the year by hitting four home runs in the first week of play. Then on April 14, he hit three home runs in one game against the Arizona Diamondbacks. Sports reporters and baseball fans followed Mark and Sammy Sosa for the rest of the year. Mark broke the record on September 8. He finished the season with 70 home runs.

Mark and Sammy Sosa remained friends throughout their home-run race in 1998.

CHAPTER 5

Mark McGwire Today

Mark had a successful 1999 season. He again took part in a home-run race with Sosa. Mark hit his 500th career home run during the 1999 season. He hit it on his 5,487th career at-bat. No one had ever hit 500 home runs in as few at-bats.

Off the Field

Mark likes to spend time with his son when he is not playing baseball. Mark married Kathy Williamson in 1984. Matthew was born in 1988. But Mark and Kathy divorced

---

Mark is still one of the best home-run hitters in baseball today.

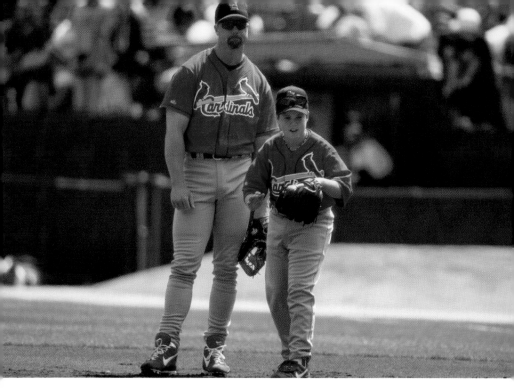

Mark's son, Matthew, sometimes works as a bat boy for the Cardinals.

after Matthew was born. Matthew now lives with Kathy and her new husband. Mark lives only a few miles away. He spends a great deal of time with Matthew. Matthew sometimes works as a bat boy for the Cardinals.

Mark also cares about other children. He visits sick children in hospitals. He helped to establish the Mark McGwire Foundation for Children. This organization helps neglected and abused children. Mark gives $1 million each year to the foundation. Mark also helps to run an Internet site through the foundation. Abused and neglected children can go to the site to find help.

Future Goals

Mark says he does not care much about individual goals. He wants to return to the World Series with the Cardinals. He says that team goals are more important to him than home runs and records.

Mark plans to stay in baseball in the future. He says that he wants to play until he is at least 40 years old. Some people believe Mark has a chance to break the career home-run record. Hank Aaron holds this record with 762 home runs. Mark might become a baseball coach when he is finished playing. He also plans to continue his work to help children.

Career Highlights

1963—Mark is born on October 1.

1981—Mark graduates from Damien High School.

1983—Mark sets the PAC-10 home-run record with 32.

1984—Mark helps the U.S. Olympic team win a silver medal. He is drafted in the first round by the Oakland A's.

1986—Mark begins his major league career. He hits his first major league home run on August 25.

1987—Mark is named American League Rookie of the Year. He hits a rookie record 49 home runs.

1989—Mark helps the A's defeat the San Francisco Giants in the World Series.

1990—Mark wins the Gold Glove award.

1995—Mark becomes the career home-run leader for the A's with 277.

1996—Mark hits his 300th career home run.

1997—Mark is traded to the St. Louis Cardinals. He hits 58 home runs.

1998—Mark breaks Roger Maris's single-season home-run record of 61. Mark finishes the season with 70 home runs.

1999—Mark leads the major leagues with 65 home runs. He hits his 500th home run in the fewest at-bats of any major league player.

Words to Know

bonus (BOH-nuhss)—a sum of money paid to a player for signing a contract

contract (KON-trakt)—an agreement between an owner and a player; contracts determine players' salaries.

free agent (FREE AY-juhnt)—a player who is free to sign with any team

nutrition program (noo-TRISH-uhn PROH-gram)—an eating plan to make sure the body is strong and healthy

professional (pruh-FESH-uh-nuhl)—someone who is paid to participate in a sport

rookie (RUK-ee)—a first-year player

strike (STRIKE)—to refuse to work until a set of demands are met

To Learn More

Dougherty, Terri. *Mark McGwire.* Jam
Session. Minneapolis: Abdo, 1999.

Molzahn, Arlene Bourgeois. *Sammy Sosa.*
Sports Heroes. Mankato, Minn.: Capstone
Books, 2001.

Muskat, Carrie. *Mark McGwire.* Baseball
Legends. Philadelphia: Chelsea House,
1999.

Savage, Jeff. *Mark McGwire, Home Run King.*
Minneapolis: Lerner Publications, 1999.

Useful Addresses

Major League Baseball
Office of the Commissioner of Baseball
245 Park Avenue, 31st Floor
New York, NY   10167

Mark McGwire (fan mail)
c/o St. Louis Cardinals
Busch Stadium
250 Stadium Plaza
St. Louis, MO   63102

**National Baseball Hall of Fame
  and Museum**
25 Main Street
P.O. Box 590
Cooperstown, NY   13326

Internet Sites

CNN/SI—Mark McGwire
http://www.cnnsi.com/baseball/mlb/ml/players/
   3866/index.html

ESPN.com—Mark McGwire
http://espn.go.com/mlb/profiles/profile/3866.html

Major League Baseball
http://www.majorleaguebaseball.com

St. Louis Cardinals
http://www.stlcardinals.com

Index